Azure AI Fundamentals

Study Guide and Practice Questions
for the Microsoft AI-900 Exam

David Voss

VOSS.AI

AI for All™

FIRST EDITION

ISBN: 9798671153989

www.voss.ai

Introduction

Audience

We created this study guide for those interested in gaining a foundational knowledge of the Microsoft Azure Artificial Intelligence services. It provides you with the information you need to pass the Microsoft AI Foundations exam (AI-900). You do not need a programming or mathematical background to read this book.

Additional Online Resources

VOSS.AI provides you with additional online resources for your studies. Specifically, you can find further study questions for the AI-900 exam. We will add new items for AI-900 and the other Azure AI exams frequently.

About the Author

David Voss has worked in IT since 1996. He began his career as a Microsoft Certified Systems Engineer, implementing and supporting various Microsoft systems. David then focused on LAN, WAN, and Data Center consulting for large businesses and Internet Service Providers. He obtained many Cisco Routing and Switching certifications, including Cisco Certified Internetwork Expert. More recently, David grew an appreciation for the transformative nature of Artificial Intelligence in the IT industry. He believes anyone who wants to learn AI should have the opportunity to do so and created VOSS.AI with that mission in mind.

About VOSS.AI

AI for All™ VOSS.AI creates products and services for anyone who has an interest in learning about Artificial Intelligence. We have chosen Microsoft AI as our platform of choice because Microsoft has made a concerted effort to ensure their AI products are accessible to those new to the field.

Study with Confidence

VOSS.AI is committed to the integrity of the exams, as well as you as a student. This study guide does not contain any material that compromises the integrity of any Microsoft exam. All materials, including practice questions, were developed using the syllabus for the exam and thorough research of published articles.

Table of Contents

Chapter 1 - Identify Features of Common AI Workloads

In this chapter, we will identify the features of the following:

- Prediction/Forecasting Workloads
- Anomaly Detection Workloads
- Computer Vision Workloads
- Natural Language Processing
- Conversational AI Workloads

Prediction/Forecasting Workloads

The hallmark of Prediction/Forecasting workloads is when your data has two available options (e.g., yes/no, true/false). AI can learn to associate historical patterns with future outcomes. You would typically use the Prediction/Forecasting model to answer either/or questions. Here are a few examples:

- Which applicants are most likely to qualify for a loan?
- Which customers are likely to attend our new store opening?
- Which leads will likely purchase online instead of in the store?

Anomaly Detection Workloads

Anomaly detection workloads typically are identified by an imbalanced data set. An imbalanced dataset occurs when several observations belonging to one class are much higher or lower than those belonging to the other classes. For example, if a small percentage of transactions are fraudulent, those certainly are the anomalies that we will want to capture. Here are a few other examples of when you would be working with an imbalance data set for anomaly detection:

- Identifying network traffic that has a signature of a network intrusion
- Verifying if values entered into a system are inaccurate
- Discovering abnormal patterns in employee time reporting

One of the challenges in working with data sets for anomaly detection is that by their very nature, anomalies are rare. It can be challenging to collect a representative sample to use for modeling. There are algorithms developed to overcome the challenges posed by imbalanced data sets.

Computer Vision Workloads

Computer Vision workloads contain images. That image data can take many forms, including but not limited to digital pictures, video, multi-dimensional data from medical scanners, and multi-input video such as views from multiple cameras. With the progress and increased usage of mobile phone cameras and video, the amount of data available for vision workloads has grown exponentially. Due to the rapid availability of computing power, accuracy rates for object identification and classification have increased exponentially. Today's computer vision systems are often more accurate than humans at image analysis. Here are just a few examples:

- Evaluating images of cancerous tumors
- Facial recognition
- Environmental impact analysis of satellite images

Natural Language Processing and Knowledge Mining Workloads

The typical workload for National Language Processing (NLP) and Knowledge Mining workloads will be words, phrases, sentences, and potentially entire articles, technical publications, wiki's or books. Machine Learning is then used to find patterns to achieve a goal. For example, many universities now feed student papers into a system that can identify if the student wrote it on their own or plagiarized portions of their submission. Other examples of using NLP:

- Language translation software
- Chatbots
- Search, grammar, and spellcheck improvements
- The primary proofreader and editor for this study guide (grammerly.com)

Knowledge mining allows organizations to gain insights from content much faster than before. Historically, humans obtained information using a trained eye. By leveraging various computing capabilities, AI can do this much faster and more comprehensively. Here are a few examples:

- Identify Quality of Service information within an enormous technical article on IP voice design
- Identify entities of importance within legal documents and flag them for review
- Quickly provide the right answer to a customer question

Conversational AI Workloads

Conversational AI is a set of technologies that enable systems to simulate real conversations with humans. Conversational AI is different than the chatbots used in Natural Language Processing because it may include voice input and output. At its best, Conversational AI can engage in human-like dialogue. Therefore, the workload for conversational will consist of the same data set as NLP (e.g., words, phrases, books, etc.) and audio. For example, if patients have frequently asked, "When I can pick up my medication?" the AI system will input, learn from, and be able to provide answers to that question.

Summary of AI Workloads

Workload	Data
Prediction/Forecasting	Binary (e.g. true/false, yes/no)
Anomaly Detection	Imbalanced
Computer Vision	Images, Video
Natural Language Processing	Words, phrases, publications, wiki's
Conversational AI	Audio, words, publications, wiki's

Chapter 2 - Identify Guiding Principles for AI

A central tenant with Microsoft is responsible and ethical AI. Microsoft has multiple governance bodies to ensure they are promoting fair and secure AI solutions. The efforts are led by Microsoft's AI and Ethics in Engineering and Research (AETHER) Committee and its working groups along with Microsoft's Office of Responsible AI (ORA).

As someone who will be using Microsoft's AI platforms, they also require that their practitioners are aware of their guiding principles for responsible AI. Microsoft desires that you can describe the following considerations for AI solutions:

- Fairness
- Reliability and Safety
- Privacy and Security
- Inclusiveness
- Transparency
- Accountability

Fairness

In a world that if often unfair and biased, AI should reduce or eliminate these undesired behaviors. Bias can impact such things as credit, hiring, and customer service. People can introduce biases (intentionally or unintentionally); therefore, we should have a diversity of people developing AI. Different perspectives on the input and output of models will help ensure they are fair and unbiased in the development phase.

Reliability and Safety

AI practitioners should ensure that the systems they build are consistent with a guiding set of values and principles. These principles go beyond the theoretical but are an intentional commitment to promoting a safer world. For example, self-driving trucks, which are now regularly used in the southwestern United States, must be at least, if not more reliable than vehicles driven by the best human drivers. The development of AI models that perform image analysis should minimize errors but also clearly identify why errors may occur so the risks can be known. This includes full disclosure of risks and issues related to the AI systems.

Privacy and Security

AI relies on a large amount of data to train systems. The amount of data poses a significant challenge for both privacy and security. AI practitioners must understand where their data is coming from and take the appropriate steps to avoid corruption. For example, a malicious actor could attempt to corrupt data to ensure inaccurate or biased results. That isn't the only challenge to working with a massive amount of data. Microsoft believes privacy is a fundamental right. Data classification and proper storage for that data based on the privacy level are an essential consideration for any AI project.

Inclusiveness

AI developers need to take part in empowering all. No one should feel left out from using AI simply because of who they are or where they were born. All technologies in AI should ensure that everyone has access to use them or, better yet, to develop new AI solutions with them.

Transparency

Transparency is essential not only from a technical perspective but also from an ethical perspective. When AI developers are transparent about issues, bugs, and risks of their AI solution, it will lead to collaboration and feedback that would not have been possible if the problems were not known. AI developers should also be open and honest as to why they are using AI and what their goals are. Transparency will allow users to choose if they want to leverage the system based not just on its technical merits but its ethical values as well.

Accountability

AI developers must be accountable for how their solutions impact the world. Accountability means we do not develop AI solutions and then "throw them over the wall," ignoring the impact they are making for good or bad in the world. We should help customers and partners be accountable, following guiding principles that reflect open and honest communication. Accountability means providing solutions to the problems our AI has introduced.

More Information: *https://www.microsoft.com/en-us/ai/responsible-ai?activetab=pivot1%3aprimaryr6*

Chapter 3 – Identify Common Machine Learning Types

Identify the following machine learning scenarios:

- Regression
- Classification
- Clustering

To understand these concepts, you should first understand the difference between the various learning types: supervised, semi-supervised, unsupervised, and reinforcement learning.

Supervised Learning

With supervised learning, the dataset consists of labeled examples, and each example consists of features. In the following diagram, we train the AI model with cat data, so it learns how to identify the features of a cat. Then, with new instances of data, it analyzes features such as whiskers, ears, eyes, nose, and tail. After the features are analyzed, the output will be labeled as "cat" or "non-cat."

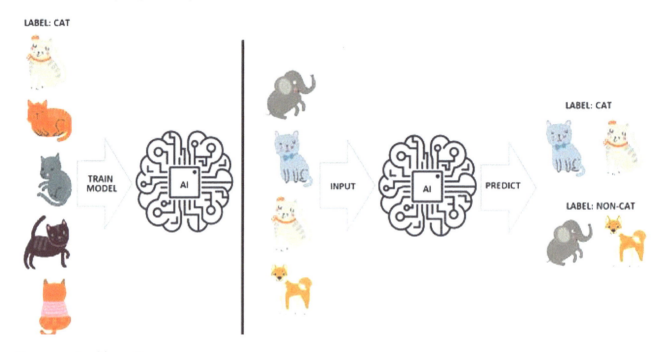

Unsupervised learning

In unsupervised learning, input data points have no labels associated with them. The algorithms used in unsupervised learning are, therefore, much different than those used in supervised learning. The algorithms attempt to organize the data to determine patterns or a structure to the data. There are no predefined rules for output. The model groups data into clusters so that the complex unstructured data has meaning and is easier to understand.

In the next diagram, unlabeled images of various animals are provided to the AI model. In training, it analyzes the multiple features of those animals (e.g., ears, tail, fur, paws, etc.). The model can then accept images of animals and find patterns within them, grouping (i.e., clustering) those with similarities. This allows you to later assign new labels to what the AI model has found, in this case, cats and dogs.

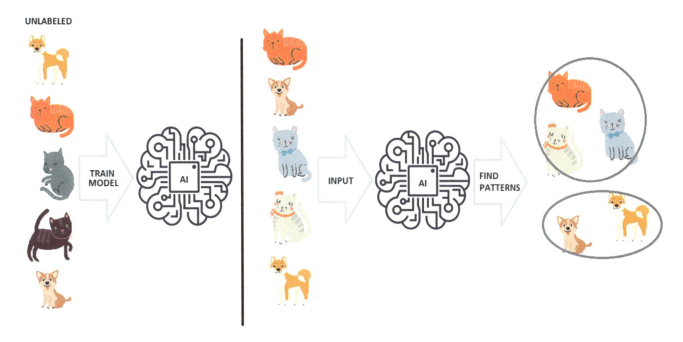

UNLABELED

TRAIN MODEL — AI — INPUT — AI — FIND PATTERNS

KEY POINT: Unsupervised learning analyzes relationships in the data and finds hidden patterns in order to define new labels.

In this diagram, you can see how Supervised and Unsupervised learning are different at the most basic level. Supervised learning takes labeled samples and creates a decision boundary between the different classes. Unsupervised learning takes unlabeled samples and looks for patterns in the data.

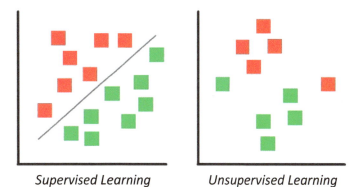

Supervised Learning   *Unsupervised Learning*

Semi-Supervised Learning

In semi-supervised learning, the dataset contains labeled and unlabeled examples. The goal is to leverage unlabeled cases to improve the reliability of the model. This improvement is often made by running the model using the labeled instances and then use the same model to run through the unlabeled cases.

Reinforcement learning

Reinforcement learning builds a prediction model by receiving feedback from trial and error. A goal (target) is defined for the model so it can know if it's improving or not. Let's use what may seem like a real life example to help get this point across. When a student goes off to college for the first time, it is a new experience where they are immersed in classes, studying, socializing, and partying, but ultimately the goal in the back of their mind is to get good grades. If the grades come back as poor, then the student learns from that, adapts their schedule to study more and party less. As their grades improve their modified behavior gets reinforced. Their adaptation to study more has worked, and that's a model they can use going forward. The same is true for reinforcement learning models. If a model knows that the goal is to label 95% of duck images correctly, then it will try various methods until it hits that 95% mark.

KEY POINT: *Reinforcement learning tries to achieve a goal through random trial and error by grading the performance of each attempt.*

Now that you understand the various types learning types, let's dig even deeper with models that you must understand to use Machine Learning and to do well on the exam.

Regression

Regression models use data to predict numerical output values. For example, a regression model could be asked to use sale price, year built, number of rooms, and distance from downtown (independent predictors) to predict the cost (numerical output) of a home.

KEY POINT: *Regression uses supervised learning to predict numerical data.*

The following figure provides an example where the input is years of post-secondary education, and the output (i.e., target) is the estimated annual income as identified by the blue line.

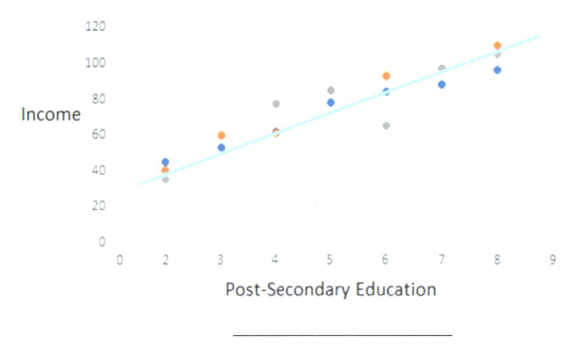

_____

FYI: The term 'regression' is attributed to Sir Francis Galton. He observed that when the heights of parents deviated from the average adult, their children tended to show less of a deviation, that is, the children 'regressed' to the average height. It was just by chance that the results showed this regression. Maybe you can think of a better name for this predictive technique?

Classification

Classification uses supervised learning to predict several values. The data is then categorized (or 'classified') using different labels, and the labels help to make predictions for the data. For example, document scanning systems that classify email attachments as either for private or for public use is an example of a classification problem. That is an example of binomial classification (output is one of two possibilities), but there is also multiclass classification (three or more).

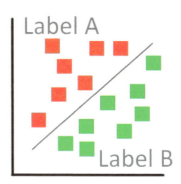

KEY POINT: Classification uses supervised learning to label data.

Clustering

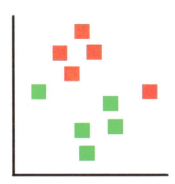

Clustering is a methodology used in unsupervised learning that partitions the data into logical groups. A single cluster will have very similar data points that make it unique from the other clusters. Clustering is a method used to derive meaning from unstructured data.

In the example on the right, the output of unstructured data clustered into two groups. It allows you to create new labels. For example, the red cluster on the top is comprised of trucks and the green cluter at the bottom is comprised of cars.

KEY POINT: Clustering uses unsupervised learning to find patterns in the data.

More Information: *https://docs.microsoft.com/en-us/azure/machine-learning/how-to-select-algorithms*

Machine Learning Scenarios in a Nutshell

Regression – "I'm going to predict using *numerical output*."

Classification – "I'm going to predict by *labeling* the output."

Clustering – "I'm going to find *similarities* in the data."

Chapter 4 – Describe Core Machine Learning Concepts

In the following section, we will identify or describe the following:

- Features and Labels in a Dataset for ML
- Training and Validation Datasets in ML
- ML Algorithms for Model Training
- Model Evaluation Metrics for Classification and Regression

Identify Features and Labels in a Dataset for Machine Learning

To identify features and labels in a dataset, we must first understand what a feature and a label is.

A **feature** is a measurable characteristic. For example, a person's facial features are their eyes, nose, and mouth.

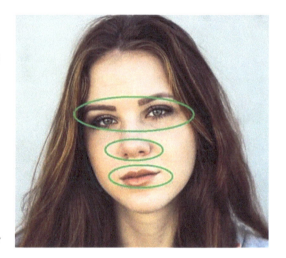

In Machine Learning, it's essential to choose the correct features when developing algorithms for classification, regression, and pattern recognition. After your model has completed training, you receive an output called a **label**.

Using the example already provided, if we fed a dataset to an algorithm, we could ask it to analyze facial features until it predicted gender. It would look at the *features* of the eyes, nose, mouth, and hair and then assign a *label* as male or female.

To break it down even further, numerical values are given to each feature analyzed: 0 = Male, 1 = Unknown, 2 = Female. If we analyze three features, then if every attribute appears to be male the score will be 0 and if every attribute appears to be female the score will be 6. Not all features will be easily identifiable so we set the model so that if the cumulative number skews high (>=4), it's labeled female, or if the number skews lower (<=3), it is labeled male.

Feature1 - Eyes	Feature2 - Nose	Feature3- Mouth	Total Score	Label
2	1	2	5	**Female**

KEY POINT: Features are characteristics that are measured to determine an appropriate label.

Describe How Training and Validation Datasets are Used in Machine Learning

A **training dataset** is a dataset that we use to train the model. A training set enables the machine learning algorithm to "learn" relationships between the features and the target variable. In supervised machine learning, training data contains known outcomes. For example, a model may learn from the training data that those who take exams in the morning score much higher than those to sit for exams in the afternoon. When the fully trained model is asked to estimate a test score, the model will know to take into account the time the test was taken.

To understand what a **validation set** is, you must first know what a hyperparameter is. In machine learning, a hyperparameter is a parameter whose value controls the learning process. It's not easy to grasp what a

 hyperparameter is, so the following example should help. One of the first things beginning violin players learn is how to tune each of the four strings on their instrument. After a while, the student begins to appreciate the melodic sound of a violin that is in tune. If the violin strings are out of tune, the student knows the song will not sound right, and therefore, they make the appropriate adjustments.

You tune hyperparameters in a Machine Learning model before applying an algorithm to a dataset just as you tune a violin before playing music. The key is to understand what hyperparameters to choose and its correct value. There is much more you can learn about hyperparameters, but this is enough to understand the concept of a validation set.

The **validation set** evaluates a given model. The evaluation is repeated to fine-tune the hyperparameters of the model. The model doesn't learn from this data; instead, the validation set results to allow us to improve upon the hyperparameters. Think of a validation set as the tuner that a violinist uses. They compare their string to the tuner to see if it is flat or sharp. In the same way, a validation set tells the Machine Learning practitioner if their hyperparameters require adaptation.

A **testing set** follows the same probability distribution as the training dataset. When a model fit to the training dataset also fits the test dataset well, minimal overfitting has taken place.

Training Set (60%) Train the Models	Validation Set (20%) Ensure models not overfitting	Testing Set (20%) Determine accuracy of the models

Describe How Machine Learning Algorithms Are Used for Model Training

Machine Learning algorithms find patterns in the training data that correlate the input data to the target. Eventually, the algorithms provide a model that captures patterns in the data and forecasts new predictions accurately. For example, let's say you want to train a model to predict if an uploaded file contains proprietary information. You would provide the ML model with the training data that contains the files for which you already know the answer (if the file has proprietary data or not). The ML model would then use this data to make predictions on new data.

In Machine Learning, there are dozens of algorithms to choose from for training, and selecting the correct one depends on many factors. Here are a few questions to consider:

- How much data is there?
- Is it a classification or regression problem?
- Is it labeled, unlabeled, or a mix?
- Is the goal for the result to predict or rank?
- Are result interpretations easy or difficult?

Select and Interpret Model Evaluation Metrics for Classification and Regression

In the same way that a student needs grades to judge their performance in school; ML models need metrics. Evaluation metrics ensure that you understand the actual performance of your model. Without metrics, you could believe that your model is performing well when, in reality, it is churning out inaccurate predictions or labels. Selecting the correct metric takes a firm knowledge of the available metrics and other key terms. Let's cover both now.

Classification Related Metrics

Classification that leverages machine learning has saturated the AI landscape. From facial recognition, spam classification to medical diagnosis, there isn't an industry that hasn't been impacted by classification. Regardless of the classification model, it requires an evaluation to ensure it is accurate. Before we discuss classification metrics, we should first understand the concept of a confusion matrix.

Confusion Matrix

Confusion matrix, otherwise known as an error matrix, is a tabular visualization of the model predictions in comparison to actual labels. Each row represents instances in a predicted class, and each column represents the instances in an actual class. The target class is what you are trying to identify. Let's review:

- TP = True Positive = Images that *were the target class* and *classified correctly* by the model as matching it.
- FP = False Positive = Images that were not the target class and misclassified by the model matching it.
- FN = False Negative = Images that *were the target* class and *misclassified* by the model not matching it.
- TN = True Negative = Images that were *not the target class* and *classified correctly* by the model as not matching it.

Actual Values

	Positive (1)	Negative (0)
Predicted Values Positive (1)	TP	FP
Negative (0)	FN	TN

In this list we break it down even further:

- TP = Target class classified correctly
- FP = Not the Target class misclassified
- FN = Target class misclassified
- TN = Not the Target class classified correctly

In the following example, we are identifying elephant images from a test set of 2000 images where 200 of them are elephant images and 1800 of them are not elephant images.

So, the target is elephants. Let's review the confusion matrix:

	Actual Values	
	Elephant	Non-Elephant
Predicted Values		
Elephant	180	100
Non-Elephant	20	1700

Out of 200 elephant images (i.e., "actual values"), the model has predicted 180 of them correctly and has misclassified 20 of them. Therefore, the predictions (i.e. "predicted values") include 180 samples predicted correctly as elephant and known as true-positive, and the 20 samples incorrectly predicted as non-elephant are false-negative. Out of 1,800 non-elephant images, the model has classified 1,700 of them correctly and misclassified 100 of them. The 1,700 correctly classified samples are referred to as true-negative, and those 100 are referred to as false-positive.

Now that you understand the confusion matrix, you can learn about metrics.

Classification Accuracy
Classification accuracy is correct predictions divided by the total number of predictions, multiplied by 100.

Classification accuracy = (true positive + true negative)/total predictions

Using the elephant example:

Elephant Classification accuracy = (180+1700)/(2000)= 1880/2000= 94.0%

Precision
When you have imbalanced data, your model could lazily predict everything as one class and still have a high accuracy rate. For example, if you have 100 images and 98 of them are dogs, if your algorithm simply predicts everything is a dog, its accuracy rate is 98%. This obviously would provide a false sense of confidence in the model. To avoid that type of situation, we need a different kind of metric to measure performance for imbalanced data.

Precision is a metric that works well with imbalanced data.

Precision= True_Positive/ (True_Positive+ False_Positive)

The precision of Elephant and Non-Elephant class in above example can be calculated as:

Elephant Classification Precision = 180/(180+100) = 64.3%

Non-Elephant Classification Precision = 1700/(1700+20)= 98.8%

The model is more precise in predicting non-elephant samples versus elephant samples, which should not be surprising since the model has seen many more examples of non-elephant images than elephant images.

Recall
The recall metric is the fraction of samples from a class that is correctly predicted by the model.

Recall= True_Positive/ (True_Positive + False_Negative)

Therefore, for our example above, the recall rate of elephant and non-elephant classes can be found as:

Elephant Recall = 180/200= 90%

Non-Elephant Recall = 1700/1800= 94.4%

F1 Score

In some instances, you will want to use both recall and precision, which can be done by combining them into a single metric. A popular metric for doing this is called the F1-score.

F1-score= 2*Precision*Recall/(Precision+Recall)

So for our classification example the F1-score can be calculated as:

Elephant F1-score = 2*0.9*0.64/(0.9+0.64)= 74.8%

There is a correlation between precision and recall of a model. If you make recall high, you will see the precision drop and vice versa.

Sensitivity and Specificity

Sensitivity is the percentage of actual positive cases predicted as true positive. These calculations should look familiar since sensitivity is also known as recall. Sensitivity is calculated as:

Sensitivity = (True Positive)/(True Positive + False Negative)
Elephants_Sensitivity = 180 / 180 + 20 = 90%

Specificity is the proportion of actual negatives predicted as true negative and is also known as the false-positive rate. It is calculated as:

Specificity = (True Negative)/(True Negative + False Positive)
Elephants_Specificity = 1700 / 1700 + 100 = 94.4%

Summary of Classification Metrics

CLASSIFICATION ACCURACY = (TP + TN)/TOTAL # OF PREDICTIONS
PRECISION = TP/ (TP+ FP)
RECALL = TP/ (TP+ FN)
F1-SCORE= 2*PRECISION*RECALL/(PRECISION+RECALL)
SENSITIVITY = TP/TP+FN
SPECIFICITY = TN/TN+FP

ROC Curve

Probabilistic models predict the probability of something being true and using our example, the likelihood of a sample is an elephant. The threshold values, that is, the values that specify whether something is an elephant or not, determine the label.

For example, if our model predicts the probabilities that five different images are an elephant, it will be labeled an elephant depending on our threshold setting. As you will see in the following

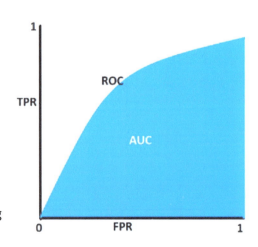

chart, how you define the cut-off (.5, .6, .7, .8) has a significant impact on whether or not something is labeled as an elephant (1 = elephant, 0 = not an elephant).

Image	Probability an Elephant	Cut-off .5	Cut-off .6	Cut-off .7	Cut-off .8
1	.55	1	0	0	0
2	.67	1	1	0	0
3	.25	0	0	0	0
4	.87	1	1	1	1
5	.71	1	1	1	0

The ROC curve is displayed after plotting the true positive rate (TPR) against the false positive rate (FPR) using various threshold settings. A ROC curve helps with model performance by enabling you to pick an excellent cut-off threshold for a model.

AUC

The area under the curve (AUC) displays the aggregated performance of a binary classifier. It calculated the area under the ROC curve and expressed the calculation as a number between 0 and 1. The AUC is the probability that the model will rank a random positive example higher than a random negative sample. The higher the AUC, the better the model is.

For the following two terms, MAE and MSE, it's not important that you memorize the exact formula, but you should know the basic attributes of each calculation.

MAE

Mean absolute error (or mean absolute deviation) finds the average absolute distance between the predicted and target values.

MSE

For MSE, just remember that it stands for 'Mean squared error,' and it finds the average squared error between the predicted and actual values. The square root of MSE is RMSE, which shows the average deviation in your model between predicted and target values (e.g., predicted house prices versus actual selling price).

KEY POINT: MAE finds the average absolute distance and MSE finds the average squared error.

Chapter 5 – Identify Core Tasks in Creating a Machine Learning Solution

The following section we will describe common features of the following:

- Data Ingestion and Preparation
- Feature Selection and Engineering
- Model Training and Evaluation
- Model Deployment and Management

Data Ingestion and Preparation

Data ingestion is the method in which data is extracted from a source or sources and prepared to train machine learning models. Unfortunately for many of us who just want to see the results, data ingestion is very time-intensive, especially in an ideal scenario where you have access to a lot of data.

When performed manually, data ingestion takes exponentially more time to prepare the data. Automation of this task is essential not only to save time but to ensure the most recent data is available for analysis. Many applications leverage machine learning to infer information about ingested data. Yes, this means using machine learning to prepare data for machine learning. Here are some of the preparation processes that these systems can automate:

- Given a local table, infer the best global table fit.
- Infer synonyms for data normalization. For example, understanding that "Dr," "Dr.," "Doctor," and "Ph.D." all mean the same thing.
- Detect duplicate records. For example, "Mr. David Howard Voss," "DH Voss," "Davidhvoss," and "D. Voss" are the same person.

Here are just a few examples of preparing your data (either manually or automatically):

- Convert categorical data to numerical: Many machine learning models require categorical data to be in a binary format. For example, if you have a column with labels containing either "cat" or "non-cat," you may want to work with a shortened labeling method such as 1 for a cat and 0 for a non-cat.
- Change data types - Using the correct data types can maximize your computing resources. For example, ensuring the zip code column is an integer.
- Address missing data – How you handle this will depend on your model. In some cases, you may remove the field without skewing the results, but in some cases, you may have to address the missing data to ensure you don't create bias in your model.
- Converting timestamps: Sometimes, date and time formats can vary considerably, especially if those who input the data could choose the format. You will need to modify the data to one format, such as YYMMDD or MM/DD/YYYY.
- Remove unneeded rows or columns – Just because we have large amounts of data doesn't necessarily we want to analyze all of it.
- Remove unwanted characters: Certain characters do not allow the data to be processed appropriately, such as spaces, carriage returns, currency symbols, and other symbols.

Feature Selection and Engineering

Feature selection is the process of selecting pertinent and suitable features to use in building an analytical model. It is the process by which you prune the field of data down to the most valuable inputs, which in turn improves training performance. You can leverage Azure Machine Learning Studio algorithms that use feature selection and engineering in the training process. The algorithm will decide what the best inputs are.

Keep the following in mind when performing feature selection:

- Add feature selection to your experiment during testing, which will inform your decision when choosing which columns to use.
- Remove feature selection from your experiment when the model is operationalized.
- Run feature selection periodically to confirm the best features.

Feature selection is different from *feature engineering*, which focuses on creating new features out of existing data. In the example provided below, if you are working on a model for a travel website, you may use feature engineering to convert the date and time field to holiday (1) or non-holiday (0) format. You are, in essence, engineering a new feature from the data.

Raw Date Data	Holiday Format (New Feature)
07042020	1
07052020	0
07062020	0

Filter Based Feature Selection

Filter based feature selection is so-called because you are choosing the relevant columns which enable you to build the best scores to build your predictive model. Columns with poor feature selection scores can be left in the dataset and ignored when you create a model. Microsoft has a variety of tools for this function. Your choice of a filter selection method will depend on what type of data you have.

Input: Dataset
Output: Filtered Dataset with feature selection scores

More information: https://docs.microsoft.com/en-us/azure/machine-learning/studio-module-reference/filter-based-feature-selection

Fisher Linear Discriminant Analysis

Fisher Linear Discriminant Analysis is also known as discriminant function analysis, and it the act of classification by distributing things into groups, classes, or categories of the same type. It discovers a linear combination of features that characterizes or separates two or more classes of objects or events.

The algorithm will determine an optimal combination of input columns that both separates each group of data and minimizes the distances within each group. The result is a compact dataset of features that can be applied to another dataset.

Input: Dataset
Output: Transformed features

More information: https://docs.microsoft.com/en-us/azure/machine-learning/studio-module-reference/fisher-linear-discriminant-analysis

Permutation Feature Importance

Azure Machine Learning Studio has a Permutation Feature Importance module. Feature values are randomly shuffled one column at a time. You measure the performance of the model by using standard metrics (described earlier in this study guide). A score determines the performance of the model with the more essential features having a more significant impact on the shuffling process and thus, resulting in higher importance scores.

Input: Trained model or test data
Output: Feature importance

More information: https://docs.microsoft.com/en-us/azure/machine-learning/studio-module-reference/permutation-feature-importance

Model Training and Evaluation

In the training process, the algorithm analyzes the data and develops patterns used for making a prediction. It's important to note that in the training process, rows with missing values are skipped. One way to address this is to use the Azure ML Clean Missing Data module before training. Another pertinent module is the Edit Metadata module, which fixes issues within the data, such as adapting column names or changing data types.

Choosing the Right Trainer

The method that you use to train a model will depend on the type of data the model requires and the kind of model itself. Study the following list of training modules to understand which one is the right one to use in each scenario:

- Sweep Clustering: Determines the ideal settings for a clustering model.
- Train Clustering Model: Trains a clustering model.
- Train Anomaly Detection Model: Trains an anomaly detector model.
- Train Matchbox Recommender: Trains a Bayesian recommender using the Matchbox algorithm.
- Train Model: Trains a classification or regression model.
- Tune Model Hyperparameters: Determine the ideal parameter settings for regression or classification model.

You may not be sure of the ideal parameters to use when training a model. In this scenario, you should use a module to perform this task for you.

- Tune Model Hyperparameters: Performs a parameter sweep on classification and regression models and then returns the best model.
- The Sweep Clustering module: For use with clustering models, will train on data while automatically detecting the best parameters.
- The Cross-Validate Model module: Provides metrics (instead of a model) to determine the best model.

Evaluate

You evaluate a model to determine whether the predictions are accurate and whether overfitting occurs. Overfitting occurs when analysis corresponds too closely to a particular set of data. When that occurs, that analysis will likely fail to predict future observations accurately.

Microsoft Azure has an evaluate category with the following modules:

- Cross-Validate Model: Select this module when you want to test the validity of your training set and the model.
- Evaluate Model: Uses standard metrics to evaluate a scored classification or regression model.
- Evaluate Recommender: Provides an evaluation of the accuracy of the recommender model.

Model Deployment and Management

The deployment of machine learning models is the process for making your models available in production environments, where they can provide predictions to other software systems. Only once models are deployed to production do they start adding value, making deployment a crucial step.

What does a deployed model look like? In essence, it's a software library that can be accessed either via a client application or within a server-side environment. You must understand that models will require frequent tuning so you must choose an environment that will allow for these updates, but an environment with SLA's that will allow for routine changes.

Since processing power is key to the success of machine learning or AI in general, the cloud is ideal for deployment. The cloud allows access to almost unlimited computing resources such as GPU's, storage, and the ability to spin up new systems as needed. The cloud also provides access to an expanding list of microservices, libraries, containers, and frameworks that would not typically be available if hosted on-premise. With an enhanced focus on AI in general, the cloud generally is the best place to deploy your model to take advantage of the latest AI technologies.

Chapter 6 – Describe the Capabilities of No-Code Machine Learning with Azure Machine Learning

In the following section, we will describe the capabilities of the following:

- Automated Machine Learning Tool
- Azure Machine Learning Designer

Automated Machine Learning Tool

Azure Machine Learning allows anyone to create and customize models via a user interface (non-CLI). The UI is leveraged throughout the ML process until deployment. Here are a few examples:

- Visualize your data to identify trends.
- Receive insight into inconsistencies or errors within the data along with recommended actions to resolve the issues.
- Build highly accurate models by leveraging automated features, algorithms, and hyperparameter selection.
- Leverage intelligent stopping to minimize compute costs.
- Leverage built-in capabilities for classification, regression, and deep learning support.
- View metrics visualizations to help you compare model performance.

KEY POINT: It's essential to create an Azure account so that you know where to find the Machine Learning offerings from Azure. You can do so at https://azure.microsoft.com/en-us/services/machine-learning/automatedml/

There are repetitive and time-consuming tasks in Machine Learning that can be automated. The process known as AutoML can help you with this and help you build ML models that are efficient, can scale, and sustain quality results. Auto ML relieves you of the time-intensive research involved with researching, producing, and comparing models. Given a target metric (by you), Auto ML can train and tune a model. Regardless of your ML expertise, it enables you to develop a machine learning pipeline for the problem you desire to address.

Automation and simplicity do not relieve us of our responsibility to understand our model. We must know how the results are achieved. The reality is that when you present results from your model, you certainly will be asked about the process of obtaining the data.

Auto ML works by creating multiple parallel pipelines that try various algorithms and parameters. The resulting scores determine which is the better model for your data.

Using Azure Machine Learning, you will typically run your automated Machine Learning training experiments using the following steps:

1. Identify if your ML problem is a classification, forecasting, or regression problem.
2. Select if you will use Python SDK or Studio Web experience.
3. Specify the source and format of labeled training data.
4. Configure the compute target for model training (e.g., Azure, local, etc.)
5. Configure the automated machine learning parameters
6. Select which metrics you will analyze to determine
7. Submit the training run.
8. Review the results.

Azure Machine Learning Designer

Azure Machine Learning provides a tool that allows you to visually connect models and datasets. If you have ever worked with Visio, you know the advantage of being able to visually diagram processes to tell a story. In the same way, Azure Machine Learning Designing enables you to visually display and design your ML model.

Here are just a few examples of how this tool can help you with your model:

- Drag-and-drop your datasets or models onto the canvas.
- Develop a pipeline by connecting the various models.
- Leverage your compute resources via the workspace by submitting a pipeline run.
- Deploy real-time pipelines to make predictions on new data.

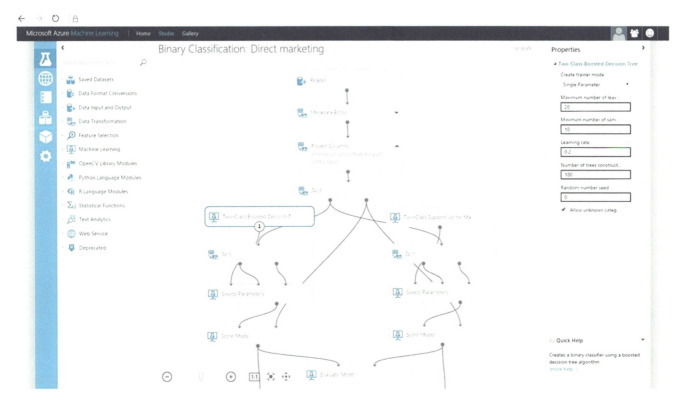

Although it is not required for the exam, now that you have already created an Azure account, you can use Microsoft's step by step guide to train and deploy a model using the Designer. Here is an excellent step by step guide to do just that: https://docs.microsoft.com/en-us/azure/machine-learning/tutorial-designer-automobile-price-train-score

More information: https://docs.microsoft.com/en-us/azure/machine-learning/concept-designer

Chapter 7 – Identify Common Types of Computer Vision Solutions

In the following chapter, we will identify the features of the following solutions:

- Image classification
- Object detection
- Semantic Segmentation
- Optical Character Recognition
- Facial Detection

Image Classification Solutions

AI is uniquely qualified to perform image classification tasks. Image classification accepts the given input images and produces output classification identifying whether something is or is not present in the image. Whether it is classifying clothing for a retailer to analyzing text and images for a crime lab or providing classification of medical images, AI removes the requirement and time it takes for manual classification or analysis. Image classification is used for a single object; for example, the image can be classified as a "cat," "truck," or "dress."

Object Detection

Object detection will find the coordinates for multiple objects found in an image while also processing relationships between images or determining if there are numerous instances of the same object in an image. For example, the output from object detection maybe, "cat, truck and dress" all within the same image.

Semantic Segmentation

Semantic segmentation goes one step farther by identifying objects at a pixel level. So, not only does this process identify that there is a "cat, truck, and dress" all within the same image, it also identifies the exact coordinates for each object, that is, identifying each pixel associated with each image.

CAT   DOG   GIRL   DOG   GIRL

Classification   Object Detection   Semantic Segmentation

Optical Character Recognition

Optical character recognition (OCR) is a technology that converts typed, handwritten, or printed text into machine-encoded text. The source is typically a document or photo. For example, a university professor may choose to use OCR to process hundreds of handwritten papers, not only to store the data digitally but also to run it through a plagiarism program to ensure the students are submitting original work.

Facial Detection

Facial detection is a technology that can identify a person from a digital image or a video frame. Typically, this is done by comparing the unique facial features in an image with a database of facial images. It does this by analyzing patterns based on the individual's facial textures and shape.

Chapter 8 – Identify Azure Tools and Services for Computer Vision Tasks

In the following section, we will identify the capabilities of the following services:

- Computer Vision
- Custom Vision
- Face
- Form Recognizer

Computer Vision API

Microsoft has an API known as the Computer Vision API, which includes Optical Character Recognition (OCR). OCR extracts text from images and documents. For example, after a bank robbery, imagine how helpful it might be for the authorities to track every single license plate that goes through the nearest intersection. Microsoft's OCR offering supports cloud, hybrid, or completely private endpoints.

The Read API can extract text from documents in seven different languages or handwritten text in English, including digits and some symbols.   It works on documents that are up to 200 pages long.

The Read API works in the following way:

1.   Upload/input the document or image.

2.   Read API accepts the image and returns an operation ID.

3.   Get Results operation: associates the extracted text with the operation ID and returns the results in the form of JSON, including confidence scores.

More information: https://docs.microsoft.com/en-us/azure/cognitive-services/computer-vision/concept-recognizing-text

Custom Vision

The Custom Vision API from Microsoft uses an algorithm to apply labels to images. Initially, you would submit a sample of images that contained or did not contain the label you desire to apply to future images. The algorithm trains using the data you provide and eventually will be able to classify new images based on what it has learned. For example, if you upload 1,000 images, and 100 of them have cats while the rest do not, the ML algorithm will train the model to learn the attributes of what a cat image contains. Once known, new images are labeled as cat or non-cat based on what was learned from the test data.

You can divide Custom Vision functionality into two features: Image classification and object detection.

KEY POINT: Image classification can apply labels to an image while object detection can identify the coordinates where the labels can be found.

More information: https://docs.microsoft.com/en-us/azure/cognitive-services/custom-vision-service/home#:~:text=Custom%20Vision%20is%20a%20cognitive%20service%20that%20lets,allows%20you%20to%20determine%20the%20labels%20to%20apply.

Face API

Azure Cognitive Services offers a service simply called "Face" that leverages algorithms to detect, recognize, and analyze human faces in images. The Face service detects and then provides coordinates of each face in the picture. In our example, it identifies the picture as a 31 year old male and even his emotions.

The *Verify API* can detect if two faces belong to the same person. There are two other API's that are helpful in this arena: The *Group API* divides a group of unknown faces based on similarity. The *Identify API* identifies a face against a database of people.

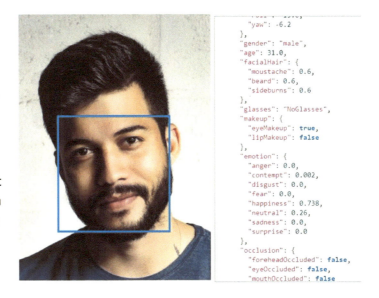

```
    "yaw": -6.2
},
"gender": "male",
"age": 31.0,
"facialHair": {
    "moustache": 0.6,
    "beard": 0.6,
    "sideburns": 0.6
},
"glasses": "NoGlasses",
"makeup": {
    "eyeMakeup": true,
    "lipMakeup": false
},
"emotion": {
    "anger": 0.0,
    "contempt": 0.002,
    "disgust": 0.0,
    "fear": 0.0,
    "happiness": 0.738,
    "neutral": 0.26,
    "sadness": 0.0,
    "surprise": 0.0
},
"occlusion": {
    "foreheadOccluded": false,
    "eyeOccluded": false,
    "mouthOccluded": false
```

KEY POINT: Know the differences between each of the API's: Face (coordinates), Verify (detect if same person), Group (finds similarities), Identify (ID against database)

More information: https://docs.microsoft.com/en-us/azure/cognitive-services/face/overview

Form Recognizer API

Azure Form Recognizer can identify and extract text and table data from documents. The input is the text from forms, and the output is structured data and relationships between the data.

Form Recognizer is comprised of the following services:

- Custom models - Extract key data from forms.
- Prebuilt receipt model - Extract data from receipts.
- Layout API - Extract text and table structures from documents.

More information: https://docs.microsoft.com/en-us/azure/cognitive-services/form-recognizer/overview

Chapter 9 – Identify Features for Common NLP Workload Scenarios

In the following section, we will identify features and uses for:

- Key phrase extraction
- Entity recognition
- Sentiment analysis
- Language modeling
- Speech recognition and synthesis
- Translation

Key Phrase Extraction

Key Phrase extraction is the task of assigning key phrases to documents to capture the main topics. Key phrases, key terms, key segments, or just keywords are the terminology which is used for defining the terms that represent the most relevant information contained in the document. Imagine if a doctor wanted to find all of the articles published in the medical school archives regarding a specific disease. Key Phrase extraction could be leveraged to quickly achieve that goal. Another example of this technology, using key phrase extraction, keywords identified from this paragraph are: key, phrase, terminology, doctor, articles

Entity Recognition

Entity recognition is the automated task of locating and classifying named entities in unstructured text into categories. The categories are predefined, such as locations, codes, quantities, etc. For example, if a Las Vegas sportsbook wanted to understand betting trends using historical data going back to 1984, they could identify such trends by classifying the data from various unstructured sources such as various betting tickets:

MGM Grand Hotel ledger reports John Doe bet $1,100 on the Milwaukee Bucks -7.5 points versus the Houston Rockets on July 17, 1989
Caesar's Palace ledger reports on 3/11/2020 Jane Doe wagered $35 on Celtics +3 v. Knicks

Which would produce an annotated text that highlights the entities of interest:

Bettor	John Doe	Jane Doe
Bet	$1,100	$35
Team	Milwaukee Bucks	Boston Celtics
Line	-7.5	+3
Opponent	Houston Rockets	New York Knicks
Date	07171989	03112020

Sentiment Analysis

Sentiment analysis uses natural language processing, text analysis, linguistics, or biometrics to quantify affective states or the sentiment of the source. Ever get frustrated on the phone when trying to deal with an automated system? It's possible, through sentiment analysis, that the system can understand your frustration and decide to send you to a customer service representative. How about that review you left on Yelp for the newest restaurant in town? It's possible the business may be scraping the Internet for data on feedback about what is or is not working, and they can then quickly adapt to ensure future customers are satisfied.

The following is an example of sentiment analysis. The overall rating for the comment is positive, although a retailer still may want to flag this one for further review since almost 1/5th of the feedback has negative connotations.

```
Overall sentiment dictionary is: {'neg': 0.165, 'neu':0.588,
'pos':0.247, 'compound':0.5256}
    sentence was rated 16.5% Negative
    sentence was rated 58.8% Neutral
    sentence was rated 24.7% Positive
Sentence Overall Rated as Positive
```

Language Modeling

Language modeling is the process of developing probabilities for word sequences. This is especially useful to voice recognition systems. If someone asked Alexa, "Where can I purchase a Harry Potter book?" the probability is that the user is asking how to purchase a book by JK Rowling, not how to purchase a "Hairy Potter" book. This is a simple example of language modeling in speech recognition, but it is also in OCR, handwriting recognition, translation, and much more.

In the following example, a university used a model to analyze the text and voice queries to the university search engines and helplines during orientation week. They realized the most popular questions were questions related to the location of the dorms and cafeteria. By using language modeling, they can ensure their search engine, helplines, and all staff can readily provide this information to students in the future. For example, when a student types in, "Where can I find" in the university search engine, the first two options for auto-complete will be 'the dorms' and 'the cafeteria.'

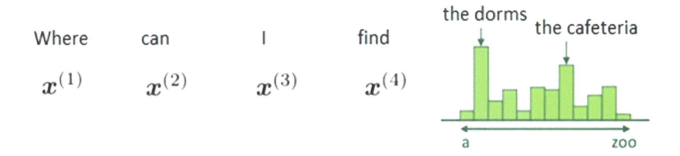

Speech Recognition and Synthesis

Speech recognition is the discipline of developing methodologies and technologies that enable the recognition of a spoken language into text by a computing system. So, if you spoke to your computer, it could type what you are saying, or if you ask Alexa for the weather, it understands that you want to know what the current weather is. Synthesis is the ability of that system to make language easily understandable. So, when Alexa responds, it should be spoken at a pace and with a nuance that feels comfortable to humans.

Translation

AI, specifically deep learning, has radically impacted language translation. The newest methods analyze the most likely translations and rank them by using statistical analysis. The translations that score the highest are closest to the training data. In a nutshell, here is how it works "under the hood."

1. Break the original sentence into segments that can be easily translated.
2. Find all possible translations for each segment using the training data.
3. Generate all possible sentences.
4. Compare all possible sentences to real sentences (from books, news, articles, etc.)
5. Score all possible sentences with the highest score being the one that best emulates real-world usage.

Chapter 10 – Identify Azure Tools and Services for NLP Workloads

In the following section, we will identify the capabilities of the following services:

- Text Analysis
- Language Understanding Intelligence Service
- Speech
- Text Translator

Text Analysis

Azure's Cognitive Services Text Analytics API provides natural language processing leveraging machine learning and AI algorithms in the cloud. The Text Analytics API provides four types of analysis:

- Sentiment Analysis - Microsoft provides analysis models that are pretrained using natural language technologies from Microsoft.
- Key Phrase Extraction
- Language Detection – The API can detect which language is input and provide a score indicating confidence level.
- Named Entity Recognition - Identify and categorize entities in your text (e.g., date/time, people, places, things, etc.)

More information: https://docs.microsoft.com/en-us/azure/cognitive-services/Text-Analytics/overview

Language Understanding Intelligence Service

Language Understanding (LUIS) leverages machine learning to predict the meaning within the text and extracts relevant information. For example, it can analyze text from applications, social media, chatbots, and any other platform that leverages natural language and responds accordingly. So, if a customer complains about the service of your restaurant on social media, LUIS can immediately extract that the service was poor and quickly respond to the customer, notifying them that a manager will contact them within the next 24 hours.

More information: https://docs.microsoft.com/en-us/azure/cognitive-services/luis/what-is-luis

Speech

The Speech API provides the following services:

Real-time Speech-to-text	Transcribes or translates audio streams or local files to text in real time.
Batch Speech-to-Text	Transcribes or translates large volumes of speech audio data.
Multi-device Conversation	Transcription and translation support for multiple clients in a conversation.
Conversation Transcription	Real-time speaker identification and speech recognition.
Create Custom Speech Models	Train custom models to meet industry specific language or environmental challenges (such as a construction site).
Text-to-speech	Converts input text into human-like speech.
Create Custom Voices	Create custom voices for your brand.
Speech translation	Real-time speech-to-speech and speech-to-text translation.
Voice assistants	Human-like conversational interfaces for applications and bots.
Speaker verification & identification	Verify and identify speakers.

More information: https://docs.microsoft.com/en-us/azure/cognitive-services/speech-service/overview

Text Translator

The Azure Translator API enables you to support multi-language user experiences. This includes language detection, translation, transliteration, and dictionaries. Translator is a cloud-based machine translation service that leverages a REST API call to translate text in near real-time.

More information: https://docs.microsoft.com/en-us/azure/cognitive-services/translator/

Chapter 11 – Identify Common Use Cases for Conversational AI

In the following section, we will identify features and uses for:

- Webchat bots
- Telephone Voice Menus
- Personal Digital Assistants

Webchat Bots

A Webchat bot is a software application used for online chat conversations with an automated system. Its goal is to provide quality information via an interface that is similar to human behavior. They are typically used for customer service or information gathering.

Welcome! What brought you here to check us out?

Just Browsing

How'd you find yourself on our site?

Im researching conversational marketing platforms

Just testing the bot

Telephone Voice Menus

A telephone voice menu, or what is commonly called an auto-attendant, is a term for a voice menu system that allows callers to obtain information or transfer to an extension without going through a receptionist. If you have ever entered "1" to hear your account information or any other key combination, then you have used an auto-attendant.

Personal Digital Assistants

A PDA is typically a small, mobile device that provides information retrieval and storage capabilities. From web-browsing, accessing email, to accessing bank account information, a PDA can give access to almost anything a computer can, while also typically allowing access to a wide array of applications. Surely you've used an iPhone, Android, or, in the past, a Blackberry device. These are all types of PDA.

Chapter 12 – Identify Azure Services for Conversational AI

In the following section, we will identify the capabilities of the following:

- QnA Maker Service
- Bot Framework

QnA Maker Service

QnA Maker is a Natural Language Processing (NLP) service that enables you to create a conversational layer over your data. For example, if someone asks a question via social media, chatbot, or speech-enabled application, your data can be queried and a response given in a natural human tone. Once a QnA Maker knowledge base is published, a client can send a question to your knowledge base and receives the results as a JSON response. It can find the most appropriate answer for any given natural language input from your custom knowledge base (KB). For example, let's say you have obtained 20 years of sales data for a large national food chain, their internal marketing team could ask a chatbot, "What were the global sales for the YumMeBurger brand from 2008-2012?". The QnA Maker service would immediately respond with that information.

Here are the steps to set up QnA Maker for your organization:

1. Create a QnA Maker resource from the Azure portal
2. Create a knowledge base (upload or leverage published information)
3. Train and Test your service
4. Publish your service
5. Continually improve your service

More information: https://docs.microsoft.com/en-us/azure/cognitive-services/QnAMaker/Overview/overview

Bot Framework

Azure's Bot Framework is a customizable web-based client. It is a seamless solution, allowing you to create a bot in just a few steps. It integrates with your website, including allowing for customization for your brand.

As you can see in the following image, interacting with a web bot is the same as texting a friend. The interface is easy to use and available 24x7. The assistant is a Machine Learning model that is continually learning more and more information based on the questions and feedback from users.

Azure's Web Chat service is configured via a simple to use web interface enabling anyone to learn, grow, and leverage this space for their company or organization.

More information: https://docs.microsoft.com/en-us/azure/bot-service/bot-builder-webchat-overview?view=azure-bot-service-4.0

Practice Questions

Congratulations on making it through the study guide. The Microsoft AI-900 exam is very straightforward. There are no trick questions. You will pass if you know the material in this study guide. The following practice exam is more complicated than the AI-900 exam because it has quite a few fill-in-the-blank questions. If you can score above 90% on this exam, even if you need to retake it 2-3 times, you can be confident that you are ready for the AI-900 exam. Good luck!

Question 1 – Multiple Choice

The hallmark of Prediction/Forecasting workloads is when your data has:

a) Two available options
b) Images
c) Imbalanced data
d) Words, phrases
e) Audio

Question 2 – Multiple Choice

The following question is best answered by which workload?

Which applicants are most likely to qualify for a loan?

a) Prediction/Forecasting Workload
b) Anomaly Detection Workload
c) Natural Language Processing Workload
d) Computer Vision Workload
e) Conversational AI Workload

Question 3 – Matching

Draw a line to match each workload to the data it uses.

Prediction/Forecasting	Audio, words, publications, wiki's
Anomaly Detection	Words, phrases, publications, wiki's
Computer Vision	Images, Video
Natural Language Processing	Imbalanced
Conversational AI	Binary (e.g. true/false, yes/no)

Question 4 – Fill in the Blank

An imbalanced dataset occurs when several observations belonging to one class are much _____ than those belonging to the other classes.

Question 5 – Fill in the Blank

One of the challenges in working with data sets for anomaly detection is that by their very nature, anomalies are _____.

Question 6 – True or False

T   F   Today's computer vision systems are often more accurate than humans at image analysis.

Question 7 – Short Answer

What workload can identify items of importance in a legal document and flag them for review?

Question 8 – Multiple Choice

What do the AETHER and ORA have in common?

- a) Semantic segmentation algorithms
- b) Archaic AI methodologies
- c) Governing bodies that promote fair and secure AI solutions
- d) Governing bodies overall AI practitioners to ensure common standards are used
- e) AI working groups that develop technical standards

Question 9 - Matching

Match the guiding principle with the behavior:

Fairness	Bring responsible for how our solutions impact the world.
Reliability and Safety	Being open and honest as to why one is using AI.
Privacy and Security	Ensuring that everyone has access.
Inclusiveness	Reduce and eliminate unfair or biased behavior.
Transparency	Ensure that the systems protect sensitive data.
Accountability	Understanding where the data is coming from.

Question 10 – Fill in the Blanks

With supervised learning, the dataset consists of _____ examples, and each example consists of _____.

Question 11 – Labeling

Put an S by Supervised Behavior and a U by Unsupervised behavior

_____ Input data points have no labels associated with them.
_____ The algorithms attempt to organize the data to determine patterns or a structure to the data.
_____ There are no predefined rules for output.
_____ There are specific expectations for the output.
_____ The model groups data into clusters so that the complex unstructured data has meaning.
_____ Input data points have labels.

Question 12 – Fill in the Blank

The following image is an example of _____ learning.

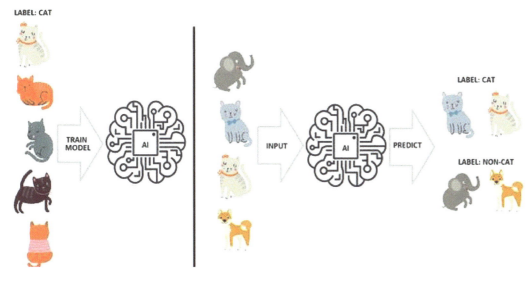

Question 13 – Fill in the Blank

Unsupervised learning analyzes relationships in the data and finds _____ to define new labels.

Question 14 – Multiple Choice

What do these diagrams represent?

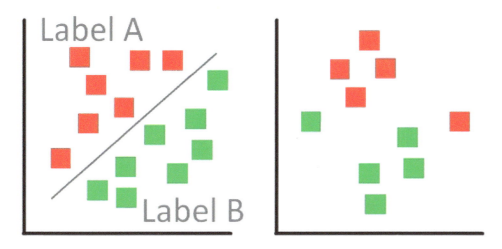

a) Supervised learning, unsupervised learning
b) Unsupervised learning, clustering
c) Regression, Supervised learning
d) Training, Prediction

Question 15 – Fill in the Blank

_____ achieves results through trial and error.

Question 16 – Multiple Choice

Regression uses _____ learning to predict _____ data.

    a) Unsupervised, numerical
    b) Supervised, labeled
    c) Unsupervised, labeled
    d) Supervised, numerical

Question 17 – Short Answer

The following chart provides an example of what type of learning model?

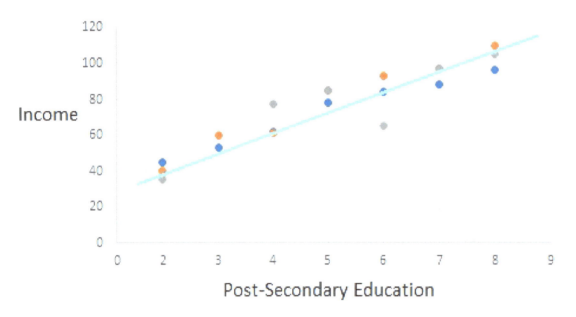

Question 18 – True of False

T   F   Classification uses supervised learning to form clusters of data.

Question 19 – True or False

T   F   Classifying images as either cat or non-cat is an example of multiclass classification

Question 20 – Matching

Match the behavior with a ML scenario.

        Regression   "I'm going to predict using numerical output."

        Classification   "I'm going to predict by labeling the output."

        Clustering   "I'm going to find similarities in the data."

Question 21 – Multiple Choice

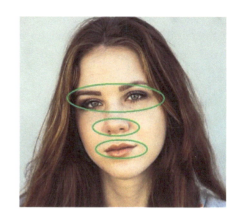

What is the best answer?

a) The labels are circled and the feature is "girl"
b) The features are circled and the label is "girl"
c) Features and labels mean the same thing and they are circled
d) The tags are circled and the feature is "girl"

Question 22 – True of False

T   F   Features are characteristics that are measured to determine an appropriate label.

Question 23 – Fill in the Blank

_____ enables the machine learning algorithm to "learn" relationships between the features and the target variable.

Question 24 – Fill in the Blank

You tune _____ in a Machine Learning model before applying an algorithm to a dataset just as you tune a violin before playing music.

Question 25 - Multiple Choice

The model doesn't learn from this data; instead, the results to allow us to improve upon the hyperparameters.

a) Training set
b) Validation set
c) Testing set
d) Production set

Question 26 – Fill in the Blank

What is the goal of asking the following questions?

- How much data is there?
- Is it a classification or regression problem?
- Is it labeled, unlabeled, or a mix?

To determine what Machine Learning _____ to use.

Question 27 – Complete the Diagram

Fill out the confusion matrix by placing the following terms in the correct location:

- Positive
- Negative
- Positive
- Negative
- TP
- FP
- FN
- TN
- Predicted Values
- Actual Values

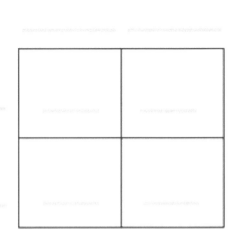

Question 28 – Short Answer

In the following example, we are identifying elephant images from a test set of 2000 images where 200 of them are elephant images.

	Actual Values	
	Elephant	Non-Elephant
Predicted Values		
Elephant	180	100
Non-Elephant	20	1700

CLASSIFICATION ACCURACY = (TP + TN)/TOTAL # OF PREDICTIONS

PRECISION = TP/ (TP+ FP)

RECALL = TP/ (TP+ FN)

SENSITIVITY = TP/TP+FN

What is the classification accuracy?

What is the elephant classification precision?

What is the elephant recall?

What is the Elephant sensitivity?

Question 29 – Multiple Choice

How does this diagram help ML practitioners?

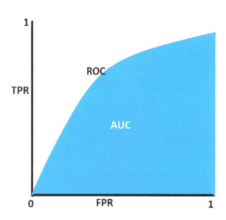

A) Helps with model performance by enabling you to pick an excellent cut-off threshold for a model.
B) Labels data
C) Helps with model performance by eliminating invalid data points
D) Helps to identify unbalanced data set

Question 30 – Multiple Choice

What calculation provides average squared error between predicted and actual values?

a) MAE
b) MSE
c) AUC
d) ROC
e) RFP

Question 31 – Matching

Match the activity with the appropriate AI pipeline step:

Data Ingestion and Preparation	The process for making your models available in production
Feature Selection and Engineering	The algorithm develops patterns used for making a prediction
Model Training and Evaluation	Selecting pertinent and suitable features
Model Deployment and Management	The method in which data is extracted and prepared to train
Feature Engineering	Developing new features out of existing data.

Question 32 – Multiple Choice

_____ is so-called because you are choosing the relevant columns which enable you to build the best scores to build your predictive model.

a) Fisher Linear Discriminant Analysis
b) Permutation Feature Importance
c) Filter Based Feature Selection
d) Classification Feature Analysis

Question 33 – Multiple Choice

_____ is also known as discriminant function analysis, and it the act of classification by distributing things into groups, classes, or categories of the same type

a) Fisher Linear Discriminant Analysis
b) Permutation Feature Importance
c) Filter Based Feature Selection
d) Classification Feature Analysis

Question 34 – Multiple Choice

_____is when feature values are randomly shuffled one column at a time. You measure the performance of the model by using standard metrics.

a) Fisher Linear Discriminant Analysis
b) Permutation Feature Importance
c) Filter Based Feature Selection
d) Classification Feature Analysis

Question 35 – Multiple Choice

Microsoft Azure a evaluate training category with the following modules. Circle all that apply.

a) Cross-Validate Model: Select this module when you want to test the validity of your training set and the model.
b) Evaluate Model: Uses standard metrics to evaluate a scored classification or regression model.
c) Evaluate Recommender: Provides an evaluation of the accuracy of the recommender model.
d) None of the above
e) All of the above

Question 36 – True or False

Azure Machine Learning allows anyone to create and customize models via a user interface (non-CLI).

Question 37 - Fill in the Blank

There are repetitive and time-consuming tasks in Machine Learning that can be automated. _____ relieves you of the time-intensive research involved with researching, producing, and comparing models.

Question 38 – Short Answer

What offering does the following describe?

- Drag-and-drop your datasets or models onto the canvas.
- Develop a pipeline by connecting the various models.
- Leverage your compute resources via the workspace by submitting a pipeline run.
- Deploy real-time pipelines to make predictions on new data.

Question 39 – Matching

Match the technique with the appropriate description.

Image classification	Accepts the given input images and produces output classification
Object Detection	Find the coordinates for multiple objects found in an image
Semantic Segmentation	Identifying objects at a pixel level
Facial detection –	identify a person from a digital image or video
OCR	Converts typed or handwritten text into machine-encoded text

Question 40 – Fill in the Blanks

Describe each Machine Learning image analysis methodology.

  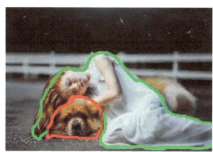

CAT   DOG   GIRL   DOG   GIRL

_____   _____   _____

Question 41 – Fill in the Blank

The _____ API can extract text from documents in seven different languages or handwritten text in English, including digits and some symbols.   It works on documents that are up to 200 pages long.

Question 42 – Fill in the Blank

The _____ API from Microsoft uses an algorithm to apply labels to images.

Question 43 – Fill in the Blank

The _____ API detects and then provides coordinates of each face in the picture

Question 44 – Fill in the Blank

The _____ API can detect if two faces belong to the same person.

Question 45 – Fill in the Blank

The _____ can identify and extract text and table data from documents.

Question 46 – Fill in the Blank

_____ is the task of assigning key phrases to documents to capture the main topics

Question 47 – Fill in the Blank

_____ is the automated task of locating and classifying named entities in unstructured text into categories.

Question 48 – Short Answer

What AI technology creates this type of output?

```
Overall sentiment dictionary is: {'neg': 0.165, 'neu':0.588,
'pos':0.247, 'compound':0.5256}
     sentence was rated 16.5% Negative
     sentence was rated 58.8% Neutral
     sentence was rated 24.7% Positive
Sentence Overall Rated as Positive
```

Question 49 – Short Answer

What AI technology creates this type of output?

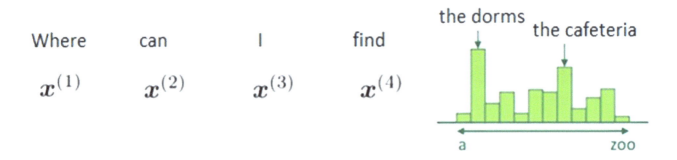

Question 50 – Fill in the Blank

If you speak to your computing system or phone, and it understands you, that is an example of _____.

Question 51 – Multiple Choice

The Text Analytics API provides what types of analysis? Circle all that apply

- Sentiment Analysis - Microsoft provides analysis models that are pretrained using natural language technologies from Microsoft.
- Key Phrase Extraction
- Language Transliteration – The API can detect which language is input and provide a score to the user indicating what language should be chosen for a task
- Named Entity Recognition - Identify and categorize entities in your text (e.g., date/time, people, places, things, etc.)
- All of the above

Question 52 – Multiple Choice

LUIS stands for:

   a) Language Understanding Intelligence Service
   b) Language Understanding Information System
   c) Language Understanding Information Service
   d) Language Understanding Information Solution

Question 53 – Matching

Match the Speech API service with the tasks it performs:

Real-time Speech-to-text	Converts input text into human-like speech.
Batch Speech-to-Text	Create custom voices for your brand.
Multi-device Conversation	Real-time speech-to-speech and speech-to-text translation.
Conversation Transcription	Human-like conversational interfaces for applications and bots.
Create Custom Speech Models	Verify and identify speakers.
Text-to-speech	Top Transcribes or translates audio streams or local files to text in real time.
Create Custom Voices	Transcribes or translates large volumes of speech audio data.
Speech translation	Transcription and translation support for multiple clients in a conversation.
Voice assistants	Real-time speaker identification and speech recognition.
Speaker verification & identification	Train custom models to meet industry specific language or environmental challenges (such as a construction site).

Question 54 – Multiple Choice

What is this an example of?

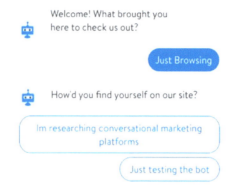

a) Webchat bot
b) PDA
c) LUIS
d) Voice Assistant
e) All of the above

Question 55– Fill in the Blank

_____ is a Natural Language Processing (NLP) service that enables you to create a conversational layer over your data.

Question 56 – Fill in the Blank

Azure's Bot Framework is a customizable _____.   It is a seamless solution, allowing you to create a bot in just a few steps. It integrates with your _____, including allowing for customization for your brand.

Answers to the Practice Questions

Question 1

The hallmark of Prediction/Forecasting workloads is when your data has:

    a)   Two available options

Question 2

The following question is best answered by which workload?

Which applicants are most likely to qualify for a loan?

    a)   Prediction/Forecasting Workload

Question 3

Draw a line to match each workload to the data it uses.

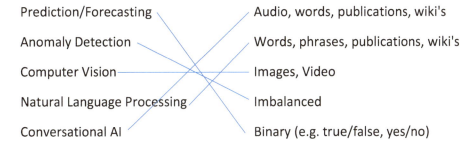

Prediction/Forecasting	Audio, words, publications, wiki's
Anomaly Detection	Words, phrases, publications, wiki's
Computer Vision	Images, Video
Natural Language Processing	Imbalanced
Conversational AI	Binary (e.g. true/false, yes/no)

Question 4

An imbalanced dataset occurs when several observations belonging to one class are much **higher or lower** than those belonging to the other classes.

Question 5

One of the challenges in working with data sets for anomaly detection is that by their very nature, anomalies are **rare**.

Question 6

[T]   F   Today's computer vision systems are often more accurate than humans at image analysis.

Question 7

What workload can identify items of importance in a legal document and flag them for review?

Answer: Knowledge mining

Question 8

What do the AETHER and ORA have in common?

    c) Governing bodies that promote fair and secure AI solutions

Question 9

Match the guiding principle with the behavior:

Fairness — Bring responsible for how our solutions impact the world.

Reliability and Safety — Being open and honest as to why one is using AI.

Privacy and Security — Ensuring that everyone has access.

Inclusiveness — Reduce and eliminate unfair or biased behavior.

Transparency — Ensure that the systems protect sensitive data.

Accountability — Understanding where the data is coming from.

Question 10

With supervised learning, the dataset consists of **labeled** examples, and each example consists of **features**.

Question 11

Put an S by Supervised Behavior and a U by Unsupervised behavior

__U__ Input data points have no labels associated with them.
__U__ The algorithms attempt to organize the data to determine patterns or a structure to the data.
__U__ There are no predefined rules for output.
__S__ There are specific expectations for the output.
__U__ The model groups data into clusters so that the complex unstructured data has meaning.
__S__ Input data points have labels.

Question 12

The following image is an example of **unsupervised** learning.

Question 13

Unsupervised learning analyzes relationships in the data and finds **hidden patterns** to define new labels.

Question 14

What do these diagrams represent?

    a)   Supervised learning, unsupervised learning

Question 15

Reinforcement learning achieves results through trial and error.

Question 16

Regression uses _____ learning to predict _____ data.

    d) Supervised, numerical

Question 17

The following chart provides an example of what type of learning model?

  Answer: Regression

Question 18

T   [F]   Classification uses supervised learning to form clusters of data.

Question 19

T   [F]   Classifying images as either cat or non-cat is an example of multiclass classification

Question 20

Match the behavior with a ML scenario.

        Regression ————————— Predicts using numerical output.

        Classification   Finds similarities in the data.

        Clustering   Predict by labeling the output.

Question 21

        b) The features are circled and the label is "girl"

Question 22

[T]   F   Features are characteristics that are measured to determine an appropriate label.

Question 23

Training dataset enables the machine learning algorithm to "learn" relationships between the features and the target variable.

Question 24

You tune **hyperparameters** in a Machine Learning model before applying an algorithm to a dataset just as you tune a violin before playing music.

Question 25

The model doesn't learn from this data; instead, the results to allow us to improve upon the hyperparameters.

        b) Validation set

Question 26

What is the goal of asking the following questions?

To determine what Machine Learning **algorithm** to use.

Question 27

Fill out the confusion matrix by placing the following terms in the correct location:

Actual Values

	Positive (1)	Negative (0)
Positive (1)	TP	FP
Negative (0)	FN	TN

(Predicted Values — row axis)

Question 28

Classification accuracy = (180+1700)/(2000)= 1880/2000= 94.0%
Elephant Classification Precision = 180/(180+100) = 64.3%
Elephant Recall = 180/200= 90%
Elephants_Sensitivity = 180 / 180 + 20 = 90%

Question 29

How does this diagram help ML practitioners?

    a) Helps with model performance by enabling you to pick an excellent cut-off threshold for a model.

Question 30

What calculation provides average squared error between predicted and actual value.

    b) MSE

Question 31

Match the activity with the appropriate AI pipeline step:

Data Ingestion and Preparation — The process for making your models available in production

Feature Selection and Engineering — The algorithm develops patterns used for making a prediction

Model Training and Evaluation — Selecting pertinent and suitable features

Model Deployment and Management — The method in which data is extracted and prepared to train

Feature Engineering — Developing new features out of existing data.

Question 32

_____ is so-called because you are choosing the relevant columns which enable you to build the best scores to build your predictive model.

      c) Filter Based Feature Selection

Question 33

_____ is also known as discriminant function analysis, and it the act of classification by distributing things into groups, classes, or categories of the same type

      b) Permutation Feature Importance

Question 34

_____is when feature values are randomly shuffled one column at a time. You measure the performance of the model by using standard metrics.

      a) Fisher Linear Discriminant Analysis

Question 35

Microsoft Azure a evaluate training category with the following modules. Circle all that apply.

      e) All of the above

Question 36

[T]   F   Azure Machine Learning allows anyone to create and customize models via a user interface.

Question 37

There are repetitive and time-consuming tasks in Machine Learning that can be automated. **AutoML** relieves you of the time-intensive research involved with researching, producing, and comparing models.

Question 38

What offering does the following describe?

Answer: Azure Machine Learning Designer

Question 39

Match the technique with the appropriate description.

Image classification————————— Accepts the given input images and produces output classification

Object Detection ————————Find the coordinates for multiple objects found in an image

Semantic Segmentation —————————Identifying objects at a pixel level

Facial detection —————————————identify a person from a digital image or video

OCR —————————————— Converts typed or handwritten text into machine-encoded text

Question 40

image classification   object detection   semantic segmentation

Question 41

The **Read** API can extract text from documents in seven different languages or handwritten text in English, including digits and some symbols.   It works on documents that are up to 200 pages long.

Question 42

The **Custom Vision** API from Microsoft uses an algorithm to apply labels to images.

Question 43

The **Face** API detects and then provides coordinates of each face in the picture

Question 44

The **Verify** API can detect if two faces belong to the same person.

Question 45

The **Form Recognizer** can identify and extract text and table data from documents.

Question 46

Key phrase is the task of assigning key phrases to documents to capture the main topics

Question 47

Entity recognition is the automated task of locating and classifying named entities in unstructured text into categories.

Question 48

What AI technology creates this type of output?

Answer: Sentiment analysis

Question 49

What AI technology creates this type of output?

Answer: Language modeling

Question 50

If you speak to your computing system or phone, and it understands you, that is an example of **speech recognition**.

Question 51

The Text Analytics API provides what types of analysis? Circle all that apply

   a) Sentiment Analysis - Microsoft provides analysis models that are pretrained using natural language technologies from Microsoft.
   b) Key Phrase Extraction
   d) Named Entity Recognition - Identify and categorize entities in your text (e.g., date/time, people, places, things, etc.)

Question 52

LUIS stands for:

   a) Language Understanding Intelligence Service

Question 53

Match the Speech API service with the tasks it performs:

Real-time Speech-to-text	Converts input text into human-like speech.
Batch Speech-to-Text	Create custom voices for your brand.
Multi-device Conversation	Real-time speech-to-speech and speech-to-text translation.
Conversation Transcription	Human-like conversational interfaces for applications and bots.
Create Custom Speech Models	Verify and identify speakers.
Text-to-speech	Top Transcribes or translates audio streams or local files to text in real time.
Create Custom Voices	Transcribes or translates large volumes of speech audio data.
Speech translation	Transcription and translation support for multiple clients in a conversation.
Voice assistants	Real-time speaker identification and speech recognition.
Speaker verification & identification	Train custom models to meet industry specific language or environmental challenges (such as a construction site).

Question 54

What is this an example of?

   a) Webchat bot

Question 55

QnA maker is a Natural Language Processing (NLP) service that enables you to create a conversational layer over your data.

Question 56

Azure's Bot Framework is a customizable **web-based client**.   It is a seamless solution, allowing you to create a bot in just a few steps. It integrates with your **website**, including allowing for customization for your brand.

After You Pass the AI-900 Exam

If you believe this study guide helped you pass the AI-900 exam, please consider leaving a review on the website where you purchased it. This study material will evolve as the AI-900 material changes but also based on user feedback. If you believe we can make this book better, please contact the author directly with your suggestions at dhvoss@voss.ai.

VOSS.AI

AI for All™

www.ingramcontent.com/pod-product-compliance
Lightning Source LLC
LaVergne TN
LVHW060159050326

832903LV00017B/366